Grandkids Say the Cutest Things

Karen O'Connor

Guideposts

New York

This Guideposts edition is published by special arrangement with Harvest House Publishers.

All Scripture quotations are taken from The Holy Bible, *New International Version® NIV®*. Copyright © 1973, 1978, 1984, 2011 by Biblica, Inc.™ Used by permission. All rights reserved worldwide.

Cover design by Dugan Design Group, Bloomington, Minnesota.

Cover illustration © Dugan Design Group

Published in association with the Books & Such Literary Agency, 52 Mission Circle, Suite 122, PMB 170, Santa Rosa, CA 95409-5370, www.booksandsuch.biz.

GRANDKIDS SAY THE CUTEST THINGS
Copyright © 2011 by Karen O'Connor
Published by Harvest House Publishers
Eugene, Oregon 97402
www.harvesthousepublishers.com

ISBN 978-0-7369-4318-5 (pbk.)
ISBN 978-0-7369-4319-2 (eBook)

All rights reserved. No part of this publication may be reproduced, stored in a retrieval system, or transmitted in any form or by any means—electronic, mechanical, digital, photocopy, recording, or any other—except for brief quotations in printed reviews, without the prior permission of the publisher.

Printed in the United States of America

20 19 18 17 16 15 14 13 12 11 10 9 8 7 6 5 4 3 2

For all the grandkids—
of any age—
who make us feel so grand!

"Children's children are
a crown to the aged."

PROVERBS 17:6

Acknowledgments

The author wishes to thank these men and women for sharing the cute things their grandkids have said to them or what they've overheard in conversations.

Rhonda Abellera • Niki Anderson • Kim Bangs • Karen Boerger • Sharon Burke • Penelope Carlevato • Mary Ann Chaussee • Vickey Powell Crim • Annetta Dellinger • Peggy Dickerson • Barbara Donner • Mary Ann Fisher • Nona Flemming • Charles Flowers • Janet Kobobel Grant • Emily Garr • Heidi Heath Garwood • Jim Gordon • Sylvia Gould • Nick and Bev Harrison • Terry Haugen • Dave Hicks • Roy and Billie Hoffman • Diana and Jerry B. Jenkins • Virelle Kidder • Kathy Landrum • Carol Nicolet Loewen • Kathi Macias • Mary Elizabeth Gibson Martin • Janet Holm McHenry • DiAnn Mills • Janice Mitchell • Celia Organista • Yvonne Ortega • Susan Titus Osborn • Dick Osborn • Barb Palmer • Christine Petzar • Becky Phillips • Rachael Phillips • Judy Scharfenberg • Vonda Skelton • Ronna Snyder • Carla and Dave Talbott • Sandra Victor • Carrie VomSteeg • Sue Watson • Janet Wolke

Contents

About the Author

Karen O'Connor is a sought-after speaker, writing consultant, and an award-winning author of more than 70 books, including *Gettin' Old Ain't for Wimps* and *Gettin' Old Still Ain't for Wimps* (more than 290,000 combined copies sold). She's appeared on national radio and television programs such as *The 700 Club, 100 Huntley Street,* and *Lifestyle Magazine.*

Joy

I never anticipated how much I would enjoy being a grandparent. The journey has been a joyful surprise that continues to delight and bless me. Are you having a similar experience? I know many grandmas and grandpas are because they've sent me the cute things their grandkids have said throughout the years. Perhaps you're one of those proud and happy grandparents. I hope so!

I'm sure you'll enjoy these endearing—and sometimes profound—insights, and I hope you'll share them with friends and family. Grandkids do say the cutest things! They keep us smiling, chuckling, and remembering with love.

If you'd like to share special moments you've experienced with one of your grandkids that might be used in a future book, please write to me at

karen@karenoconnor.com

I look forward to hearing from you!

Karen O'Connor

Part I

Paying Attention

As grandparents, we can be sure of one thing: Our grandchildren pay attention—in many cases better than we do. They are watching us, and they let us know it. They are plain talkers. We find out what's what by listening to them, discover new horizons by finding out their likes and dislikes, and even grow some by taking their advice from time to time.

> "Grandma, you'd look a lot better if you cut your hair. Long hair doesn't work on older women."

Off to the beauty shop I go.

> "Grandpa, no climbing on ladders. Did you know a man your age fell off the

roof while hanging Christmas lights?
He lost his balance and splat! He broke
a leg and an arm."

Oh my! Grandkids not only say *cute* things; they
also say *truth* things. We still have a lot to learn, even
though we're w-a-a-a-a-a-y up in years—according to
our offsprings' offspring. As we teach our grandkids a
thing or two, they are teaching us as well. I, for one, am
choosing to pay attention. How about you?

> *You, LORD, keep my lamp
> burning* (Psalm 18:28).

Here or There?

Vonda lives in South Carolina, while two of her grandchildren live in Florida. When visiting, she sometimes needs a little help finding her way around their neighborhood. One evening while walking with her three-year-old and six-year-old grandkids, she stopped at an unfamiliar intersection. Her grandson pulled her hand to continue.

"Just a minute," Vonda said. "I'm trying to figure out where I am."

Six-year-old Garrett stretched up to her ear, cupped his hand around his mouth, and whispered loudly, "MaMa, you're in Florida."

Taking Credit

Niki's granddaughter often accompanies her daddy to the post office. While walking home, little Zoe carries the junk mail. One day her father opened an envelope with a credit card and an application to activate it. He handed it to Zoe to carry home, where he would toss it into the trash.

Zoe instantly brightened and said, "Thanks, Dad! Now I can buy my own candy."

Eyes to See

Mimi DiAnn had extensive eye surgery one year, just a few days after Christmas. On New Year's Eve, she and her husband babysat their grandchildren while the young parents enjoyed a night out.

Three-year-old Grace's mother had prepared the little girl for the boo-boos on Mimi's eyes. She didn't want the child to be traumatized when she saw her grandma's bruises.

That night while Grace and Mimi were brushing their teeth before bed, Mimi looked in the mirror and nearly scared herself! "Grace, your Mimi really looks ugly tonight," she said.

Grace stopped brushing, removed her toothbrush from her mouth, and placed her hand over her heart. "Oh, Mimi, you're not ugly!" she exclaimed. "You're like the Grinch who stole Christmas. You have a big heart."

It's All In a Name

Jonathan's father, Dean, referred to his wife as "Mamma."

One day three-year-old Jonathan corrected his father. "Daddy, she's not your Mamma. Grandma Gibbs is."

Grandma Gibbs pointed to Dean and asked, "Jonathan, is *that* Daddy?"

"Yes," he said. "He's called Dean."

Card Shark

Jerry and Diana's seven-year-old grandson, Sammy, announced one day, "Dad, I've got a joke for you. What kind of animal do you *not* want to play cards with?"

His father thought about it and then replied, "I don't know. What kind?"

"A cheetah!"

"That's funny, Sam!" his dad said. "Do you know why that's funny—and why you don't want to play cards with a cheetah?"

"Yeah!" Sammy announced quickly. "Because they eat people!"

True Love

When four-year-old Russell and his grandmother Rhonda spend time together, they refer to it as "Mimi Day."

At the end of one such visit, Russell declared unexpectedly, "Mimi, I love you so much. I just want to live with you forever. I don't ever want to go home."

Grandma Rhonda was sure in that moment the boy loved her more than anyone else in the world! How special. But then she felt bad because his parents totally loved him.

"Russell," she said tenderly, "you know how much Mimi loves you, but you do have to go home. You belong to your mommy and daddy, and they'll miss you if you stay here."

Rhonda drove him home, still delighted over Russell's statement yet saddened at the same time. Once they walked through the door, Russell ran to his mother.

"Mommy, I missed you so much! And I love you so much!" With that, he jumped into her willing arms and hugged her tightly.

Rhonda stood there, chuckling to herself. Russell certainly knew how to wrap the ones he loved around his little finger.

Thanks, I Think!

Eleven-year-old Janie looked her grandmother up and down, providing fashion points as the two dressed for dinner and a movie.

"Grandma," Janie commented with a satisfied look, "you look like a teenager—except for your face...and your hands...and..."

"You can stop after the word 'teenager,'" Grandma interrupted with a laugh.

Duh!

Six-year-old Carson told his grandmother in great detail about a book he was reading at school.

"One of the characters in the story didn't even know what was going on," he said, arms folded across his chest as he rolled his eyes. "And Gramma," he added, "it was *so* obvious!"

No Pointing

Gran observed her granddaughter interacting with the girl's father.

"Patty," he said to his young daughter. He then pointed to a bottle of ranch salad dressing at the far end of the dinner table.

Patty looked at Dad and said patiently, "Use your words, Dad."

Easy Living

One day Grandma Becky was running errands in Santa Cruz, California, where she lives. Her five-year-old grandson, Lance, was with her at the time.

"I thought I would talk to him about working with his hands when he is older," Becky said. "When he is ready to make money and eventually earn a living. So I asked, 'Lance, how do you make money?'"

At first Lance didn't understand her point, so his grandmother explained, "How would you make enough money so you have what you need to buy things?"

Lance paused for a moment and then responded. "You stand on a street corner and hold a cardboard sign in your hands."

Grandma Becky broke out laughing. Santa Cruz has a number of homeless people on the street, and some do stand on corners holding signs requesting money. Apparently they had made quite an impression on her grandson.

Please Don't Change

As Mary Ann hugged her granddaughter Taylor, age three, she bumped the little girl with her eyeglasses. Fearing she might have hurt the child, she said, "I think I'm going to get contacts so I won't bump you when I hug you."

"Oh, Nana, please don't get contacts," begged Taylor, "'cause then you wouldn't look like my nana."

Sight to See

The first time Mary's granddaughter Angie camped in a tent beside a lake, the girl woke up in the morning, looked out the window, saw the white-capped waves, and shouted excitedly, "Look, Mommy! See all the white towels floating on the water!"

Not the Marrying Kind

When Janae was visiting Carol and Jerry, Carol took the opportunity to turn a conversation about marriage she was having with her husband into a teachable moment. "I mentioned to Janae how important it is to marry someone you really like being with," said Carol.

Suddenly the three-year-old raised both hands, palms facing Carol. "Stop! I don't want to talk about marrying."

Carol made another comment about marriage, and again Janae's hands went up.

"I told you. I don't want to talk about this anymore." End of subject!

Happy Birthday

The pastor at Doug and Christine's church was giving the children's sermon one Sunday. He was talking about Christmas being a celebration of Christ's birthday. Trying to relate this to the kids' world, he asked if they sang songs at birthday parties. Quickly he sang a few lines of "Happy Birthday to You" very quietly to give them the general idea.

At that point, one child piped up with impeccable timing, "Yeah, but we don't sing it that fast."

The entire congregation burst out laughing.

Game Plan

At age three, Marnee wanted to buy a new game while she shopped with her grandma.

But Grandma said, "You'd better put it back. You don't know how to play it."

Marnee had a ready response: "*I* know how to play it. I just need some help—'cause I don't know how to play it."

Tall Tail

While almost home from a long road trip with the family in tow, Luke's dad, Nathan, was getting irritated by a driver behind him following too close. Thinking all of the kids were asleep in the backseat, he said, "I wish that idiot would get off my tail!"

Luke quietly and matter-of-factly stated, "Dad, you don't have a tail."

Call Me Uncle

Dave's sister planned her wedding around the time he was old enough to be ring bearer. Some time later in her marriage, the young woman announced she was expecting a baby. Everyone was very excited for her, and the conversation turned to whether she'd have a boy or a girl.

Hearing family members talk, Dave put in his two cents' worth: "I sure hope they have a boy because I'd rather be an uncle than an aunt!"

Nothing New Here

A friend was looking at a picture of Micah standing with the evil queen from *Snow White* while at Disneyland.

"She looks kind of mean," the friend said to Micah. "But in the picture you don't even look scared."

As straight-faced as could be, Micah replied, "Nah, I'm used to bad girls."

Planning Ahead

"Grandpa, did you go on dates with girls when you were a teenager?" asked nine-year-old Randy.

"Sometimes, like to a dance or a movie. Why do you ask?"

"I want to be ready when I'm a teen."

"Do you have anyone in mind?" asked Grandpa.

"Maybe Leah, but she'll have to get her braces off first."

Dial 911-NANA

Nana Virelle is convinced her 15-month-old grandson, nicknamed "Thane," is a genius. After awakening from his nap, and with a fresh diaper in place, he toddled after his mom toward the bathroom. Noticing the coveted cordless phone lying on the hall floor, he picked it up and pressed two buttons "7" and "#," walked into the bathroom, beaming I'm sure, and handed the phone to his mom, who had just washed her hands.

"Thane, who did you dial?" his mom, Lauren, asked, chuckling. "This will be interesting," she said aloud as she listened to the ringing in the phone.

Three hundred fifty miles away, Thane's nana rolled over from a brief afternoon nap to answer the phone. "Hello, Kidders' residence," she said and heard shrieks of laughter from the other end.

"Thane just dialed you, Mom! I can't believe it. How did he do it?" Lauren managed to get out as she continued to chuckle.

Virelle said she wondered why her daughter was surprised. "The child just needed his nana. I was soon on my way for a visit!"

Just Too Much

Blake, age six, and his friend were overheard talking about families and babies.

"I don't think I'll ever get married," declared Blake, "because marriage and babies are a lot of work."

Are You Serious?

Linda's granddaughter faced a difficult family situation when she was very young. Her mother thought counseling might help. During one of the counseling sessions the doctor asked Cyndi if she took any medication.

"Yes," Cyndi replied.

"What is the reason for taking the medicine?" asked the doctor.

"To get well, silly," she replied.

Big Guy

Jim took his grandson Keith sturgeon fishing when the boy was ten. Everyone in the boat was excited when the boy hooked what felt like a big one. As they took turns helping Keith reel in the fish, it jumped partway out of the water several times, giving everyone a thrill.

After a half hour, when the sturgeon was almost next to the boat, Keith turned to his grandfather. "Grandpa! It's bigger than my brother!"

"We all laughed and agreed with him," said Jim, "since Keith's brother, James, was fourteen years old and probably around 5'8" at the time. The sturgeon Keith landed was 6'2"!

Since the huge fish was over the legal limit, they measured it and let it go. "But we always smile big when we share the memory at family gatherings," Jim shared.

Part 2

Sweet Sayings

Sometimes our grandkids melt our hearts with their sweet spirits, warm words, and thoughtful gestures. I remember when my father died, my granddaughter Shevawn was five years old. She had an uncanny empathy toward my mother, even though she didn't know her well. Shevawn was sitting next to Mom during the church service. She slipped her little hand into Mom's frail one. Then she turned to me and whispered, "Wherever Great-Grammy's hand goes, mine goes." And so it went until we were ushered out of the building after the service. What a precious memory.

One of my friends was lamenting the fact that she was growing old even as her grandchildren were growing up. She hated to see the time passing so quickly. She shared her concern with her 11-year-old grandson, Paul.

"You don't look old to me," he said matter-of-factly.

"You just look like a grandma's supposed to look. I like you that way."

She suddenly felt better!

We do matter—more than we might imagine. If we sow sweet words, we'll reap the same. Let's keep doing it.

A heart at peace gives life to the
body (Proverbs 14:30).

Pride and Joy

Seven-year-old Shelby joined her grandparents for their church's Christmas program, which consisted of a "living tree" of 150 choir members, including her grandpa. Afterward she told everyone around her, "My grandpa is a Christmas tree, and I'm his little ornament."

That Hurts

At just over two years of age, Jordan got a spanking for something he did. He didn't cry though. He looked at his mama and said, "You hurt my feelings!"

Sweet Tooth

Marnee's grandmother's church collected candy to give to orphans in Mexico. When Grandma explained to her granddaughter who the candy was for—children who don't have mamas to buy it for them, Marnee sympathized.

"Oh, poor children," she said.

The next day she asked if the church was going to give all the candy to the "orphants."

A New Experience

How was school today?" Tyler's grandma asked the little boy at the end of his first day of school.

"Good."

"Tell me about it," coaxed his grandmother.

"I didn't take a lunchbox," he said. "I ate a ham-and-cheese sandwich in the cafeteria. And you know what else, Nana?"

"No, what?"

"I had an apple—and it even had the peel on it!"

Nothing Could Be Finer

Susan and her husband took their nine-year-old grandson, Kolton, with them to visit his cousins over a long weekend. They stopped at Coco's coffee shop on the way to Merced, California, for a break during the drive. They ate dinner at a Marie Callender's restaurant on the way home. Both eateries had kids' menus that offered a main dish and dessert. Kolton substituted a Caesar salad for the regular salad at both meals.

Several weeks later, the boy spent the night with his grandparents again. Susan and Dick took him to a movie, and as they walked past a familiar café featuring hamburgers, Susan paused.

"Kolton, that used to be one of your favorite places. Do you want to go there for dinner?"

"No thank you, Grandma," he said. "That was before you introduced me to the finer things in life."

Your Turn

Robert, your birthday present from your Aunt Mona Lisa and Uncle Lucien will be late," explained his grandmother. "But PaPa's and mine will arrive on time. Just think! You can do a happy dance when your gift arrives."

Robert replied just before heaving a big sigh, "MeMa and PaPa, you're retired. *You* do the happy dance."

Inside and Out

Emily's eldest granddaughter went to the doctor for a checkup before school started. As she and her mom were driving home, granddaughter Taylor commented, "The doctor never asked me about my feelings, and they get hurt too."

Emily commented that she'd like to see a notice in the doctor's office that reads: "Feelings checked here."

Fishing Line

Nana Mary Ann took grandson Zach, age three, to a fishing pond on a damp day in October. Everyone else was busy, so it was just the two of them. "We'd gone to the live bait store to get minnows and red worms," reported Nana. "Then we stopped at the grocery store so Zach could pick out a snack. He chose grape juice, potato chips, Nutter Butter cookies, Reese's Pieces, and a banana, which he held in a bag as we walked and then he put it beside him as we sat by the side of a small levee. He looked adorable in his blue jeans, red hoodie sweatshirt, and little rubber boots.

"Later he clutched the Spider Man rod and reel I had purchased for his birthday as I showed him how to thread the red worm on the hook. He played with the worms in the bucket, took the minnow net and tried to catch the small fish, and then sat back down on the muddy bank.

"Then he said thoughtfully, 'Nana, it just doesn't get any better than this.'"

First Day, Best Day

The first day two-year-old Allison went fishing with her brother and grandmother, she declared, "Nana, this is the first day of the rest of my life!"

Tyler laughed and rolled his eyes. "You mean this is the best day of your life."

"Yes! This is the best day of my whole life!"

Nana winked at Tyler and whispered, "All two-and-a-half years of it."

Tyler chuckled.

Broad Shoulders

Eight-year-old Noah and I went camping with other kids and their parents and grandparents in the Anza Borrego Desert one autumn weekend. I was feeling nostalgic as we climbed to the top of a large outcropping of rocks and perched ourselves on the edge to gaze at the beautiful scene in front of us.

"Noah, I hate to think of the day when I'll be too old to hike up here," I commented.

"Don't worry," he replied, placing a protective arm around me. "I'll just sling you over my shoulder and carry you to the top."

Not All for the Money

Eleven-year-old grandson Charlie did some chores for his grandparents in order to raise money for a trip to Orlando, Florida, with his Pop Warner football team. After working very hard for about five hours, he told his grandmother his true motive: "Grandma, I do it 75 percent for love and 25 percent for the money."

What a great attitude!

Close Enough

It was three-year-old Easton's first year of preschool. His older brother, Caden, had started two years earlier. A few days into the semester, Caden got into the car at the end of the day and told his mom, "Easton was sitting at a table all by himself at lunch."

Their mother was concerned. "Easton, why were you sitting by yourself at lunch?" she asked.

"Because I wanted to sit as close as I could to where Caden sits," the younger brother replied.

Da Best!

Ronna's three-year-old granddaughter, Hannah, was struggling with pronouncing her "G's." Whenever she tried, a "D" slipped out instead.

"Damma?" Hannah said.

"Yes, Hannah?" Grandma replied as she waited expectantly.

"You da best Damma in da whole wold!"

Ready Reader

Steven, at age five, asked his grandma one day as he pointed to some small print in a publication, "Can you read that without your glasses?"

"Not if it's printed really small," Grandma answered.

"Oh well," Steven replied. "I can't read at all. You're lucky."

Not a Problem

Sylvia's granddaughter Marnee, age 18 months, was still learning to pronounce the letter "B." So the dog named Bobo was called Dodo. But when an older brother, Tim, announced, "She can't say her B's," Marnee looked at him and said "B" as clear as a bell!

Road to Heaven

Sharon's grandson Luke inquired of his father, "Dad, where is heaven?"

His dad admitted he didn't know exactly.

Luke came to his rescue. "If I go to heaven you can use your GPS to find it and come visit me."

Part 3

Taking Charge

I had fun assembling this section. Some grandkids make it so obvious that they're in charge—at least in *their* minds. They'll threaten to run away if things don't go well for them, even though they might not go very far.

They also have big plans for the future—such as shooting all the bad guys or winning all the games they play—especially the ones with you. And sometimes they can be quite demanding.

I like their flashes of assertiveness and the belief that they can be anything they want to be. Many of us lost that vision for ourselves somewhere along the way. Perhaps our grandchildren can help us rekindle it if we stay close to them and tap into their unlimited resources of imagination and wonder.

Grandkids can be bossy one minute, submissive the next; hold you at arm's length one day, and collapse on your lap the day after that. They cry easily and laugh uproariously. Most of all they are authentic—at least the young ones are. And we can help the older ones hang on to their true selves by showing them who we really are.

Humility is the fear of the LORD;
its wages are riches and honor
and life (Proverbs 22:4).

Take Your Pick

Annetta's three-year-old granddaughter, Megan, watched her newborn sister, Kirstin, nursing at her mother's breast. Megan turned to Grandma and announced, "One is for chocolate milk, and the other is for orange juice."

My Room!

Twelve-year-old Mairin gave her girlfriend a tour of our house during a recent visit. When she came to what we call "the guest room," Mairin declared with certainty, "This is my room."

High Tech

Six-year-old Isabella and four-year-old Zoe live in London, so their grandparents talk to them and read books with them on Skype. One day, as Grandma finished reading a storybook to Zoe, the little girl discovered that dinner was ready.

Just like that she said, "I'm going to un-Skype you now, Grandma. Goodbye."

Click.

Perplexed, Grandma turned to her husband. "I've been un-Skyped, and I didn't even know that was a word."

Like It or Not

Grandma and Grandpa were camping with their grandkids. The eight-year-old was ordering her Grandpa to do a million things. After a while he finally asked, "Who do you think I am, Cinderella?"

His granddaughter didn't miss a beat. "Yes, and I'm the wicked stepmother!"

Taking Charge

When Ronna's grandson, Justus, was about four years old, he spoke up during a Sunday school lesson on Daniel in the lions' den.

"What would you do if you were in a den of lions?" the gentle teacher had asked her students.

Justus, who comes from an Idaho family of avid hunter–gatherer types, thought long and hard and then waved his hand with vigor. "I know what I'd do!" he declared when his teacher called on him. "I'd get my dad's gun and shoot the suckers!"

For Girls Only

Grandma Sandy arrived at her daughter's house, and three-year-old Daniel met her at the door. He noticed she had a gift in her hands.

"It's for Mommy's birthday," Sandy told him.

Daniel looked up at his grandmother. "Is it a girly-girly gift?" he asked.

Sandy laughed. "Yes, Daniel. It's a girly gift. Would you like to give it to her for me?"

"Sure! Did you get it at Sephora?"

Sandy could hardly believe that a little boy could be so well versed in shopping for women's things that he even knew the name of one of his mom's favorite stores.

When his mom came into the room, Daniel handed her the gift and jumped up and down waiting for her to open it. She did. It was a pair of sparkling diamond earrings.

Daniel took one look and yelled, "It *is* a girly gift, Nana!"

Mom and Nana had a good laugh.

Risky Business

"Gramma, do you want to know what I'm going to be when I grow up?" asked Ryan.

"Sure, what's that?"

"A spy."

"Really?"

"Yeah. I'm going to spy on the bad guys."

"Sounds dangerous. What do you like about that job?"

"You get to use guns!"

"Oh my, Ryan. That's dangerous, don't you think? I wouldn't like that kind of work."

"I know," Ryan responded. "Girls don't, but boys do."

The Old Man Is Snoring

Little Janae, three years of age, stayed overnight with Carol and Jerry. About 2:30 in the morning, Jerry awakened with a start and then tapped Carol.

"Janae's awake," he said, pointing to the child standing at the foot of their bed.

"What's wrong, honey? Can't you sleep?" Jerry asked. "Am I snoring?"

"Every minute!" she responded.

Pipe Down

Marisa, age three, became impatient and irritated with her four-month-old baby sister, who often cried.

"No thank you for the noise, Lyndsi!" she'd say.

On one occasion the two girls were settled for the night—or so their mother and grandmother thought. As Grandmother Barbara and her daughter were enjoying a nice visit, they heard a sudden yell from Marisa: "Mom! I'm asleep and Lyndsi's awake!"

Jumpin' Jack

Jack, age two, challenges himself to do what his siblings and cousins can do. When he succeeds he says, "I told you!" At one point, he was trying to get the courage to jump off the big diving board into the swimming pool.

"I can jump off the diving board like they can!" he said over and over. Finally he did it, and then he popped up out of the water and joyfully exclaimed, "I tooooooold you!"

Rescue Man

At a family get-together, Grandma served dishes of ice cream to the adults and gave ice cream bars to the kids. Her three-year-old grandson ate his treat and then talked his grandmother into a dish of ice cream. Later, when the adults and older kids were playing a game, he came running into the living room hugging the ice cream container to his chest.

"Grandma!" he shouted. "The ice cream fell out of the refrigerator, and I saved it. Can I have some more?"

He got his third helping of ice cream.

Movin' On

Janet's grandson Josiah, age four, argued with his mom about taking a bath. He wanted to continue playing with his toys. Exasperated, he said, "I'm going to run away."

"Josiah," his mother said, "that makes me very sad. Where would you go?"

"To Wal-Mart," he said firmly. "They have toys there and nice ladies."

Germ Warfare

Carla's grandson Micah sobered when his mother told him not to share his water bottle with his friend.

"Why? Do I have a cold?" asked the three-year-old boy.

His mom explained that everyone has germs, so it's best to use your own cup.

Immediately Micah grabbed a blanket, lay down on the couch, and covered himself.

"What's wrong?" asked his mother.

"I have to lie down," he said, "'cause I have a germ."

Good Idea

Grandpa Ben, a part-time sign language instructor, invited his three grandkids over for an afternoon. When the noise level became too much, he had second thoughts.

"Please pipe down!" he called to the trio in the den. "I can't even hear myself think." Between the computer, the CD player, and the shouting back and forth, he was ready to ship the siblings home to their parents.

Eight-year-old Bradley came in and faced his grandfather with a sheepish grin. "I have a good idea. Teach us sign language, and then we can talk to each other without disturbing you."

One-stop Shopping

Lani took her granddaughter grocery shopping with her. Little Regina started ordering Grandma when to stop and when to go. She wanted to linger in the toy aisle. Her grandma indulged her but didn't buy anything.

When they reached the produce section, Regina said, "Let's go, Grandma. It's taking too long!"

Basket Case

Luke's grandfather was refereeing a fourth-grade girls' basketball game, and Luke and Grandma sat in the stands watching. As his grandpa ran back and forth and back and forth, officiating, Luke looked up and asked his grandmother, "What team is Papa on, anyway?"

All Mine

One of the bright spots in Nick and Bev's lives is their ability to visit with their faraway granddaughters via Skype. Since they live in another state, the grandparents don't get to see them as often as they'd like, so they visit via webcam approximately once a week.

Recently, when the girls and their mother called Bev over the web, four-year-old Emma piped up. "Mommy, can you please go away so I can talk to Gram by myself?"

"It sure made me feel like a million dollars to know she wanted me all to herself!" Bev said.

Part 4

Celebrity Status

Some grandkids are natural grandstanders. They're ready to grab the microphone, sing a song, play a tune, or put on a show. Others like the limelight too, but they get the jitters before the curtain goes up. When it's over, though, what fun to take a bow and catch a bouquet of flowers.

It's been fun for my husband and me to attend the events that feature our grandchildren. You probably feel the same way. I like seeing the kids carry on the family traditions of song and dance and acting. There's nothing quite like the stage to build self-confidence and self-expression—even though it can be scary at times.

Not every child is a ready performer. Some like to watch and clap and memorize the storyline and song lyrics…or praise those who are out there doing their thing. Still others enjoy fame by association or creating their own recognition by declaration.

> *You will be blessed when you come in and*
> *blessed when you go out*
> (Deuteronomy 28:2-6).

It's Who You Know

Judy's eight-year-old granddaughter, Madelynne, was excited about her solo in her school's talent show. She'd been anticipating this night for weeks. She looked darling in her shiny top, black leggings, and sparkling pink flip-flops.

As she fidgeted from one foot to the next, in true stagehand style her grandmother applied her blush and glittering eye shadow. She then whispered into her granddaughter's ear, "You look like a rock star."

Madelynne gave a big, confident smile and said, "Grandma, when I'm famous I'm going to give you a backstage pass."

Line Starts Here

Six-year-old Miles was chosen for a part in the school play. He was excited but also apprehensive. He was already so popular with the boys and girls in his class that he sometimes felt overwhelmed when his mom or grandma dropped him off in the morning. Everyone crowded around him and shouted, "Hi, Miles!"

"Now, it'll be worse than ever," he explained to his grandmother. "Everyone's gonna want my autograph."

But he went through with it anyway.

Of course, his grandparents lined up for an autograph too.

Protection

Grandma Yvonne bought her grandson, Brian, two and a half years old at the time, a dress suit and then took him and his mom to lunch at an elegant restaurant. The tables were decorated with fine linen, fresh flowers, china, and silverware. Brian ordered his favorite drink, apple juice, which the waiter delivered.

Then the little boy told his grandma and mom that he had to go to the bathroom. Apparently he was feeling protective of the drink—not wanting anyone to take it while he was gone. He got up and then turned back to the table.

"Grandma," he said, "I need to spit into my apple juice so no one will drink it when Mommy takes me to the bathroom."

Grandma grinned and said, "Don't worry about it, Brian. I'll spit in it for you."

Brian liked that idea!

My Team

A four-year-old boy who lives on a farm was watching the "March Madness" basketball games with his family. As soon as he saw a team with green and yellow outfits he announced, "That's the John Deere team!"

Name Dropping

Grandma Janice took Ellery, then two and a half years old, to a "Disney on Ice" program. When the princess skated into the arena, Ellery popped up and shouted, "I know her! She's on my Pull-Ups."

New State

Grandpa James was helping his young granddaughter Hannah learn the map of the United States.

"Now repeat after me," said James, pointing to the various states with a finger. "This is California, Oregon, Nevada, and Utah."

Hannah proudly copied his lead: "This is California, Oregon, Nevada, and Mytah."

Royalty

Dick and Susan took their children and grandchildren to church for the Christmas program. When the first wise man entered the back of the church, Susan pointed him out. "Look at the king!"

The six-year-old stood up on her seat and shouted, "Where's the queen?"

The congregation had a good laugh.

Part 5

Oh Say Can't You See?

Have you ever noticed that grandkids have eyes to see and ears to hear—whenever you don't want them to or when you least expect it? They let you know too!

> "Didn't you see the stop sign, Grandpa? I saw it." *I'll bet you did.*

> "Didn't you see my friend's house when you turned the corner? It's right there." *But I've never been to your friend's house before.*

> "Looks like I won at checkers again. Didn't you see my strategy?" *No, I guess I missed it.*

> "Looks like my feet are bigger than

yours. Did you notice?" *So that's why you haven't borrowed my boots lately.*

However, their observations are usually good ones. They keep us on our toes and in our right mind!

> *You desired faithfulness even in the womb; you taught me wisdom in that secret place* (Psalm 51:6).

Singing the Blues

Bobbie took her grandson Max on an excursion to pick blueberries. She thought it would be the perfect follow-up to their reading the charming children's book *Blueberries for Sal* by Robert McCloskey. "Afterward we'll make a blueberry pie together," Grandma Bobbie said.

Max nodded and smiled, so Bobbie was certain she'd chosen the perfect outing.

Later in her kitchen, after the pie was cooling on the counter, Bobbie poured two glasses of milk and pulled out plates for pie.

"None for me," Max said. "I'll have some chocolate chip cookies."

"What? After all we did to finish this pie?" Bobbie was floored.

"I don't like blueberries," Max said. "Don't you remember?"

"No. Why didn't you remind me?" Bobbie asked.

"I thought you wanted to spend time with me, so I kept my mouth shut."

Where's Mom?

Christine and her husband, Doug, were visiting a museum with Doug's granddaughter Anna, about seven years old at the time. They were looking at a display of Victorian-style dresses. Knowing Anna's mother loved these ornate designs, Grandma Christine said, "I can really see your mother in that dress."

Anna leaned in closer to the glass, squinted, and said, "I don't see my mother in that dress."

English, Please!

Carla and Dave's grandson, Micah, at age three and a half, saw a bunny in a field. He asked his mom how to say the word "bunny" in Spanish since the family lives in Mexico. She didn't know the answer but suggested they talk to their friend Joe who is fluent in the language.

With a "duh" tone in his voice, Micah replied, "No, Mom! Joe doesn't speak bunny."

Slow Down

Four-year-old Kolton was invited for a sleepover one Friday night at his grandparents' house. He and Grandpa Dick decided to go out for ice cream after dinner in Dick's Porsche. When they returned, Kolton was wide-eyed.

"We really went fast in Grandpa's race car!" he exclaimed.

A little later he confided to Grandma, "I see why Grandpa has to go to school to learn to drive slower."

Dick was scheduled to spend the next day in traffic school for a speeding ticket.

Voice Change

Poppy sat in his favorite chair in front of the television. He was grousing about something he saw on the news.

Seven-year-old Peter walked in, looked at his grandfather, and said, "Grandpa, you need a voice lift."

Poppy touched his wrinkled face. "You mean a face lift, don't you?"

"No, a voice lift."

"What's that?" asked his grandfather.

"Getting a new tone of voice. Instead of complaining, start being grateful."

Poppy smiled. Hadn't he said something similar to Peter some time ago?

Big Bird

Four-year-old Mikey was watching *Sesame Street* with Grandma.

"You look like Big Bird," Mikey asserted.

"I do?" Grandma was curious about what she had in common with the large yellow Muppet character.

"You both smile nice, and you have big tummies."

Sorry, You Lose

Max and his grandpa played the little boy's favorite board game, "Sorry," whenever they were together. After Grandpa lost three or four games in a row, Max looked up.

"Sorry, Grandpa. Looks like you're just a loser."

Modern Art

Six-year-old Jason liked to draw and paint. Everyone in his family encouraged him. Grandma Debra even gave him a gift certificate for six lessons with a local art teacher. One day while visiting his grandmother, Jason handed her his latest picture of a countryside with tall pine trees and a stream running through it.

"It's lovely," she said. "I'm so proud of you. I'll put it on the fridge right away."

Jason held up his hand. "No, Grandma. I made this so you'd have something really pretty. Take down that ugly picture over the sofa and put up mine."

Compu-Smart

Bev works on a computer all day long so she's very electronic literate. She can also program the cell phone, television, DVR player, and even her digital alarm clock. But her five-year-old grandson, Joshua, outshines her in the tech department.

"When my husband, Nick, and I babysit, Joshua tells me how to turn on the TV, tune into the Xbox or the DVR so we can watch a movie, where the movie is in progress, and then how to return the TV to normal programming when the boys go to bed. He assures me that 'everyone knows how to do this, Gram!'"

Gram admits she is twelve times older than Joshua, but he is a hundred times smarter than she is.

Part 6

Teen Grandkids
Are Creative Too!

I couldn't put together a book of grandkids' sayings without including a few comments made by teenagers. Teens have a way of putting it out there—sometimes right in our faces. As long as they're respectful I can take it. I like to know what they're thinking and how they see life.

They are also a huge help, *when we ask*. They can whip up a cake, fold a basket of laundry, climb a ladder without losing their balance, and organize photos on the computer.

But watch out. They'll poke you on Facebook and post pictures you might prefer to toss, but you can also count on them to say "I love you!" And at that moment you'd give them the moon (and they know it).

Let us love one another, for love
comes from God (1 John 4:7).

Welcome!

One afternoon while sitting in my daughter's kitchen during a weeklong visit, my 17-year-old grandson, Jake, burst through the front door after school, paused, looked at me, and then declared, "Magah, it sure is nice to come in and see you sitting there!"

Treat Yourself

A grandma overheard her granddaughter Tess talking with her father. The teen owed her dad some money, so she handed him the bills and quipped, "Here, buy yourself something pretty."

Never Too Late

One day my almost-teenaged granddaughter Mairin and I were talking about getting together for a movie and dinner. I was lamenting the fact that soon she'd be too busy with her friends to spend time with my husband and me. Gone were the days when she'd hang out for hours at a time talking, playing games, doing homework, and reading with me before bed.

She looked at me with big eyes and said, "Grammy, that will never happen. I will always want to spend time with you and Granddad."

I was so relieved!

Late-Night Hug

One night during a visit with our grandchildren and their parents in the Midwest, I walked by my 15-year-old grandson, Liam, who was glued to the computer. I didn't want to disturb his concentration, but I did want to say goodnight. I tapped him on the shoulder.

"'Night, Liam. I'll see you in the morning."

He popped up from his chair like a jack-in-the-box and hugged me so tightly I thought I'd break—but it sure felt good.

"Goodnight, Grammy. I love you, and I'm so glad you're here."

I slept very well that night!

Tall Girl

Emerald's grandfather asked the six-foot-tall teenager to help him reach something off a top shelf.

"Sure," she replied, "*if* you call me 'Your Highness.'"

Not Bad

Fifteen-year-old Shelby was visiting her grandparents for five days, helping around the house and yard to earn some money. She and her grandmother also played board games, went swimming, and ate out for dinner a few times. At the close of the week, Shelby summarized her visit: "You're sure old, Grandma, but you're really fun!"

Get on It

Robin's 13-year-old granddaughter, Leslie, is the shutterbug in the family. She's as comfortable with a camera as she is with the family dog. When Robin purchased a new Canon she was eager to show her granddaughter what she could do.

Robin took the camera out of the protective bag and asked Leslie to pose for a few shots. Frustration set in when she couldn't see an image through the lens. She finally handed it to her granddaughter with disgust. "I can't get this to work. What am I doing wrong?"

Leslie took the camera, checked a few things, and handed it back. "For starters, Grandma," she said, "you need to turn it on."

Sing, Sing!

I t was Christmas Day, and all I wanted was to hear my 17-year-old granddaughter Shevawn, a stunning soprano, and her boyfriend, Brandon, a rich baritone, sing a couple of duets for me.

Shevawn seemed shy all of a sudden. Was this the same girl who used to perform without being asked? The one who danced across the wood floor of her family home with each of her grandfathers just a few years ago?

I gave up asking, but I must have had a yearning expression on my face because just then they began singing—one song and then two, their beautiful voices filling the living room with gorgeous sound. Next they tucked themselves behind the piano, played a couple of keys to catch the right pitch, and off they went with another lovely melody. They sang to the end without a hitch.

I was filled with emotion. I clapped and said thank you.

With that, Shevawn came over and gave me a big hug. She smiled and said, "That's your Christmas present, Grammy."

Indeed it was, and I will treasure it through all the days to come.

Promises, Promises!

Donna's 13-year-old grandson, Shawn, spent the weekend with his grandmother while his parents were out of town. At bedtime the first night, Donna kissed Shawn's cheek and said a quick prayer. "I love you," she added. "You know I'd do anything for you."

With that Shawn sat up in bed and said, "Can I cash in on that promise tomorrow? I need a new skateboard. The one I have is looking pretty dingy."

Part 7

All About God

Kids say a lot of cute things, among them comments, questions, and musings about God. How blessed we are as grandparents to watch them discover and experience His love and grace, grow in Him, and live by His guidance. As part of the process, however, they come up with some interesting theological understandings…or misunderstandings…as well as a few unique ways of praying.

I remember when I was a child in parochial school kindergarten. My teacher told us we each had a guardian angel who would look after us and help us stay out of trouble. She recommended we leave room for the angel to sit close to us during class by scooting to one side of our seats. I took her words to heart and spent the rest of the year miserable in a too-cramped space while my angel took the majority of the chair.

By first grade I caught on that "she" was a spirit and didn't need an earthbound chair to sit on. By second grade I had "learned" that my angel was content to rest on my shoulder. And by the time I graduated from eighth grade I wasn't sure any of those statements were even true.

What I did know, however, was that God loved me—always had and always will. That was enough for me then…and now. As a grandmother, I rest easy knowing God is with my grandchildren too.

The LORD your God is with you (Zephaniah 3:17).

Wedding Feast

Grandma Penny takes her three-year-old grand-daughter Elsa to Bible Study Fellowship with her. While Penny studies with the adults, little Elsa enjoys her time in the children's class. Since the moms and grandmas are learning the same stories as the children, Penny is always excited to hear what Elsa has to report when they meet at the end of the session.

"After we had studied John 2, about the wedding at Cana, Elsa said, 'Did you know that Jesus turned the water into wine at the wedding at the Stanley Hotel?'"

Penny and her daughter—Elsa's mother—had a good chuckle at that one because the Stanley is a historic hotel where Elsa's mother is the wedding director. Elsa joined in the fun.

"Well, maybe it wasn't at the Stanley Hotel," she amended.

Take That, Satan

At age four, grandson Steven proclaimed, "Jesus is gonna lock Satan in jail. He can't get out. Then there'll be no more tummy aches, and we can play all day!"

If Only...

Pondering the story of Adam and Eve in the Garden of Eden, the young grandson lamented, "I wish Adam and Eve wouldn't have done what Satan told them to do. If they hadn't, things would be so nice. We could pet the snakes and everything."

No Sweat

"Wanna hear a song my dad taught me about Jesus?" asked Miles.

"Of course," I said. "I'd love to listen to you sing."

The six-year-old ran through a couple of verses, never missing a beat or word.

I complimented him on how quickly he had memorized the lyrics.

Miles looked at me, a bit puzzled. "But it's in English," he said. "If it were in Hebrew I couldn't have done it so fast."

Place Your Order

Concerned there might not be enough spouses to go around when it was her turn to marry, granddaughter Marnee said, "The husbands are all married, aren't they? But God will make me another one."

Right On!

Allison was deep in thought. She looked at Taylor and said, "God cannot pray to Himself."

Taylor had the perfect response: "God doesn't have to pray."

Stumped!

Grandma Nancy talked with her five-year-old grandson, Miguel, about the importance of listening and obeying in order to live a happy life that is pleasing to God.

Miguel paid close attention to his grandmother and even nodded, indicating he got what she was talking about.

When she stopped speaking, Miguel sighed heavily and then remarked, "Obeying—that's the hard part."

Heavy Rain

Tyler and his grandmother went for a drive to see the effects of a local flood.

"Nana," Tyler said, "I thought God promised there would never be another flood."

"God promised there would never be another flood to cover the whole earth," Nana explained.

"It wasn't here yesterday," said Tyler. As far as he was concerned, the flood *had* covered the whole world.

Our Big God

Four-year-old Joey and his grandmother decided to make giant Bendaroo caterpillars—waxy, colorful string things. Their accompanying conversation turned theological.

Joey told Grandma he was creating the biggest caterpillar in the world—even bigger than God.

"How big is God?" asked Grandma Rachael.

Joey threw up his hands, spraying Bendaroos over a ten-foot radius. "God is 31 and 300 and thousands big! Bigger than the sun! Bigger than the sky!" he shouted.

Rachael asked if his striped purple-and-yellow caterpillar was as big as the sun.

Joey shook his head.

"Is your caterpillar as big as God?"

He shook his head again.

Grandma noticed that although some adults can't accept the fact that God's handiwork outshines their own, Joey—and kids like him—don't give it a second thought. They know God is *big*.

It Must Be Magic

One summer two grandkids were both enthralled with shiny, broken glass. One day at the park they found pieces from a car window that had shattered into zillions of reflective, iridescent shards.

Allison said, "These are beautiful diamonds. How did they get here?"

Taylor replied, "God threw them down here and made them burst."

Allison smiled. "God can do anything. I think He has a magic wand."

Bless God

Caden, age five, was saying his prayers. "Bless Mommy, bless Daddy, bless Jesus." He paused, looked up at his dad, and giggled. "Daddy, I just said 'Bless God!'"

His grandmother noticed that he'd picked up the concept that Jesus is God. She loved it.

No Arguing That

Jonathan, age three, looked at the sunset and asked, "Did God draw it, Mom? God is a nice man, isn't He?"

The Bright Side

At age four and a half, a grandson mused aloud, "When I go to heaven, I can't wait to see Grandfather all made new. I never saw him new—just when he was old."

Part 8

Pet Tales

Topsy, a little black-and-white dog, was my first childhood pet. I sobbed the day my mother said he was going to a nice big farm where he could run around and be happy all day long instead of being confined to our small yard. *Sure!* I thought. I wouldn't say Mom was lying, but I did wonder if she was breaking the news as gently as she knew how that Topsy was just too much for her to handle in addition to rearing three kids in a crowded house that our grandfather lived in with us.

Maybe that's why I let my kids have all the pets they wanted—well, almost. We had two dogs at one time, a litter of puppies, a bird, a hamster, a cat, goldfish, and a turtle, though not all at the same time. At the moment, I don't have any pets of my own, unless you count my granddog, Tanner. I take him on regular walks. We are so attached to one another that when I arrive or leave he doesn't let me out of his sight. Such love! My husband sees him as competition. My grandkids hand over the leash happily, when I visit.

"Tanner, it's Grammy. Wanna go for a walk?" they say.

He pants yes, and so we head out, Tanner and Grammy, for a walk and a doggy sniff-sniff at every bush and tree we pass.

> *You will go out in joy and be led forth*
> *in peace...and all the trees of the field*
> *will clap their hands* (Isaiah 55:12).

Prayer Rescue

Linda read preschooler Marnee a story about a cat whose kitten fell into the water while Mother Cat led her litter across a bridge.

Marnee stopped the story and announced she would pray for the kitten—which she promptly did. "Kitty be all right now," she stated, ready for the story to resume.

Food Stealer

Grandma Janet shared this cute saying from her grandson Sean, four years old at the time. While the young boy and his mother checked out some items at the grocery store, including a large bag of dog food, the clerk attempted to make conversation with the child.

"What kind of dog do you have?" he asked.

Having heard the dog often described in a certain way, Sean quickly answered, "A moocher."

Take It Slow

Granny, guess what?" said four-year-old Lisa while speaking on the phone.

"Tell me!" Granny responded.

"We have a pet."

"You do? That sounds exciting. What kind?"

"A turtle. It doesn't bark, and it doesn't eat too much."

Good Grief

Five-year-old Shevawn was proud to show her grandparents her first pet—a cat. The two cuddled on the sofa as Shevawn lovingly stroked the tabby's soft fur.

Then one day the cat was diagnosed with feline leukemia and had to be put down. Shevawn was shattered at the thought of her beloved cat going to heaven. After days and days of crying and sadness, she went to her mother one morning.

"I'm finished grieving," she declared and proceeded to carry on with her day.

Whatever It Takes

Zach, age four, and his grandmother were pretending to fish for trout in his yard. "What kind of bait are you using?" Grandma asked. "I'm using salmon eggs."

The boy thought for a minute, and then said in all seriousness, "I'm using ham and eggs."

No Thanks!

Grandma Mary took Angela and Rodney to visit her elderly neighbor, Mr. Davis, and to see his new kittens. As they were admiring the tiny babies, the man said, "When they get big enough to eat, you may have one of them."

Angela looked shocked, stood silent for several moments, and then said with a quivering voice, "But I don't eat cats."

Big Bug

Frankie and Brad were showing their two-year-old brother a big, green, dead June bug and trying to get him to hold it.

The little boy's eyes were huge as he looked at the gigantic bug in Frankie's hand. He started to reach for it, but jerked his hand back. He tried again. Finally, terrified, he let Brad place it in his hand. His body stiffened as he tried with all his courage to hold it.

Suddenly he was sure it moved. He jumped and threw it in the air so fast the bug went flying high in the sky. Trying to build his "big boy" reputation in the eyes of his brothers, he screamed, "He jumped out! He jumped out!"

Peas, Please

Grandma invited her five-year-old grandson, Daniel, over for a "grandma and me" weekend. That evening she planned to serve roast beef for dinner. She gave Daniel a choice of vegetable.

"Would you rather have peas or carrots?" she asked.

Daniel replied with a knowing look, "Peas! Rabbits eat carrots, and I'm not a rabbit!"

Needless to say, his grandmother served peas.

Fish Gotta Swim

Heidi overheard her son speaking to his seven-year-old son, Adam. "Chickens must be mad, since they are flightless birds," stated the boy's father. "Who wants to be a bird that can't fly?"

Adam caught on immediately. "Yeah, that's like fish that can't swim."

Part 9

Not So Old...

I remember walking into a meeting for senior citizens one day after I'd turned 65. "We're in the wrong place," I whispered to my husband. "These are a bunch of old people. I'm not one of them yet!" He reminded me that, indeed, I had arrived. I might not have felt older, but my years put me in that category.

Whether or not we feel our age, our grandkids almost always have something to say about it—sometimes flattering and sometimes painful (though well-meaning). I've been reminded that I have "blue lines" on my legs when some other grandmother does not. (I don't want to meet her, okay?) Grandmothers and grandfathers have been encouraged to have surgery to correct the hooded eyelids that sometimes accompany the aging process. And leave it to a perceptive grandchild with good eyesight to notice the lone hair poking out of a grandmother's chin. I recall as a child not wanting to kiss my aunt's sister for that very reason. The ramrod hair poked me whenever she pulled me into a hug.

In addition, granddaughters take delight in giving fashion tips. "Granny, you really should get a new pair of boots...or jeans...or sweater...or jacket." (Hint! Hint!)

Okay, we might be showing our age but I believe we're showing our wisdom too.

Is not wisdom found among
the aged? (Job 12:12).

This Old House

One day while Celia's grandkids, A.J., six, and Alexis, five, were visiting, they charged through the house slamming doors. Grandma sat them down and explained that the house was very old, and if they kept slamming doors, the doors might break. Then she checked to see if they got what she said.

A.J. answered immediately. "Yes, you don't want us to slam doors because the house is old like you."

Stars and Stripes

Grandma Sue's grandson declared, "You and Grandpa aren't old—except for your hands. They have stripes."

An Old Softie

Blake, age four, described his great-grandma, age 78, to his grandma: "Nona, Great-Grandma is really old, but she is so soft."

No Worries

When Tim made a reference to Grandma soon being "over the hill," his four-year-old sister popped right up.

"If you live over the hill, Dramma, I will ride my bike and come see you."

Second Chance

Annetta, a grandmother, interviewed four-year-olds. Some of their responses brought a chuckle as well as some things to mull over. Here's one she particularly enjoyed:

"What is a mirror?" she asked one child.

"It's to tell you if you like what you see, and if you don't you start over."

Nick of Time

When her granddaughter Brittney was about five, Kathi took her to the cemetery to show her where some of her ancestors were buried. They browsed the headstones until the little girl came across one that showed the deceased had lived to 104 before she died.

"Wow!" Brittney exclaimed. "She was ready."

Hear! Hear!

You're seventy-two?" Tim asked in surprise when the family sang "Happy Birthday" to his grandmother.

"I am. What do you think?" she asked and twirled around, hoping he'd be impressed at her spontaneity and energy.

"Wow! You seem so young. I thought you were about seventy!"

Grandma Holly sighed. Two years off her age were better than two years added on. She'd take 'em.

You're Fine

Teresa drove into a handicapped parking place in front of the grocery store.

Three-year-old Katy looked at the sign. "Grandma, does that mean you're sick or old?"

"No, honey, but I have to use a cane until my knee gets better, so I'm allowed to park in this special place."

"I'm glad you're not sick or old, Grams. I like you just the way you are."

See You Later

Five-year-old Mark and his sister Jenny went to the movies with their grandparents. Grandpa complained the sound was too loud, and Grandma was having trouble with her new glasses.

Mark came up with what he thought was the perfect solution: "Grandma and Grandpa, how about waiting in the car, and Jenny and I will meet you there when the movie is over?"

Old as a Hippo

Grandma Barb and her husband went to the zoo with their grandson Ryan's preschool class one summer. Ryan's seven-year-old brother, Josh, came along too. One of the highlights for the boys was taking the miniature train ride through portions of the zoo. Grandma and Grandpa folded their "grandparent" bodies and climbed aboard. As they chugged by the hippo section, the engineer announced that at age 54, the animal on view was the oldest living hippo in captivity in a zoo.

Josh turned to his grandmother with eyes as big as saucers. "Wow, Grandma, he's older than you are!"

Grandma didn't let on that it's been awhile since she was 54!

Part 10

Good Question

On crazythoughts.com I found a long list of funny questions—some I've asked myself, some I've heard my grandkids ask, and some I've never thought of or heard before. Most were good. I've listed some of them below for your enjoyment and pondering. Asking the questions and speculating on the answers could be an interesting and enlightening exercise for you and your grandchildren. Be aware, however, that they may also lead to another question that for many grandkids never gets answered to their satisfaction: "Why?"

- At a movie theater, which armrest is yours?

- How far east can you go before you're heading west?

- When does it stop being partly cloudy and start being partly sunny?

- Can you daydream at night?

- Why is it called a funny bone when it's not funny at all if you hit it?

- Do you yawn in your sleep?

- Can you "stare off into space" when you're in space?

- If you soak a raisin in water, does it turn back into a grape?

I will praise the LORD, who
counsels me (Psalm 16:7).

Say That Again

When Lucas and his family returned from a trip to the San Diego area (including a side trip to Disneyland) to visit relatives, their grandmother asked the children where they'd gone.

"We went to Disneyland!" Burke replied enthusiastically.

"And we saw fireworks," said Conrad, adding the appropriate sounds.

"Where did you visit after Disneyland?" Grandma asked.

"We went to Sam...Sammy eggo," said Burke.

"Who did you see?" Grandma asked.

"Sammy Eggo!" Burke repeated.

I'd Rather Not Say

"MaMa," said Vonda's eight-year-old grandson as he flapped the skin hanging from her upper arm, "why is your arm like a water balloon?"

Get to the Truth

Nona remembers her young granddaughter listening intently to her and her husband talk about Antarctica. Just then she piped up with a question. "Daddy, I thought you only have one aunt—Aunt Helen?"

Sad Note

Until recently Nana Mary Ann took long drives with her granddaughters. She took the train to Tustin, met her daughter, dropped her off at work, and then drove her grandkids back to their home in Lake Forest—about half an hour's ride on the 405 freeway in Southern California.

"These rides provided a lot of time for good conversation," said Mary Ann.

Granddaughter Zoe, who is interested in everything, often asked some wonderful questions. One day she asked, "Nana, do coyotes ever smile?" She paused and then concluded, "No, I don't think so. They always sing such sad songs."

Sleep Aid

I picked up my grandson Miles from school one day when he was in first grade. I noticed he looked beat.

"Are you feeling tired?" I asked. "You look like you've had quite a day."

He'd been sick over the holidays, so I assumed he was still recovering his strength and needed more sleep.

He piped up from the backseat, "I have to get to bed earlier. For the past five weeks I've been keeping teenagers' hours."

Nighty-Night

Isabella, age five, and Zoe, age three, went camping with their grandparents after a family wedding. They'd never been in a camp trailer before. Isabella looked around puzzled and finally asked, "Where are we going to sleep, Grandpa?"

Keeping a straight face, he replied, "On the table."

"Oh, won't that be too hard?" Isabella questioned.

She was very relieved when Grandpa showed her how the table broke down and turned into a comfy bed with cushions.

Crackup

Karen B. sat down in the rocking chair and the children sat cross-legged on the floor around her in the Sunday school classroom. A little girl on the left bent over until her head nearly touched the floor. Karen's granddaughter did the same.

"Mrs. B., why do you have cracks in your feet?" asked the little girl.

Karen breathed a silent prayer for wisdom. She explained that the cold weather affected them so she kept lotion on her feet during the dry winter months. "Do you remember the story of Mary putting oil on Jesus' feet?" she asked, making use of this teachable moment.

After class as she packed up to go home, Karen's granddaughter came up to her and whispered, "Grandma, your feet are just fine."

Good Thought

One day Rachael and her four-year-old grandson were taking a walk. The boy's eye level is about belly-high on his grandmother. He turned to her, patted her small protrusion, and said, "Grandma, do you have a baby in there?"

"No, honey, there's no baby."

He thought for a moment and then added, "That would have been cool to be walking with a baby beside me, wouldn't it, Grandma?"

"Yes, honey. Very cool."

Rachael appreciated that he didn't tease her about being a bit overweight. He accepted her as she was and simply shared his curiosity.

Keeping It Even

Billie and Roy's three-and-a-half-year-old grandson, Ben, was standing with his father, Brian, looking into the refrigerator for a yogurt.

"I think I'll take a boysenberry," said Brian.

Ben looked at his dad with a quizzical expression and asked, "Is there a 'girlsenberry'?"

Waste Not, Want Not

Miles' mother and dad are surfers, as are his two older sisters. Living in Santa Cruz County, California, the surfing capital of the nation, they steal away to the beach as often as they can all year long, but especially during the summer. First-grader Miles, however, is not yet a dedicated surfer. When his mother proposed some family beach days, Miles gave his opinion in no uncertain terms.

"Mom, why are you wasting all my time at the beach when I could be playing with my friends?"

It Tingles

At age eight, Frank needed some teeth filled so his grandmother took him to his Uncle Rodney, a dentist.

On the way home, he said, "Nana, my mouth feels really funny. It's all tingly."

"Yes, it will feel like that for a while because Uncle Rodney gave you a shot to make your mouth go to sleep so it wouldn't hurt when he put in the fillings."

"Uncle Rodney said I have bugs in my mouth. I think he wears goggles when he works on my teeth so if they fly out when I open my mouth, they won't get in his eyes."

"They're not real bugs, honey. What do you think they look like?"

"I think they look like ladybugs." He thought for a moment and then said, "Nana, if I have one in my mouth and if I bite it, will it go to sleep?"

Two by Two

While visiting my daughter Erin and her family one year, I invited six-year-old Shevawn to a movie. Her mom thought it would be nice if all three of us could go together, but Shevawn squashed that idea right away.

"Mom, I need a little private time with Grammy, okay?"

So off we went—just the two of us.

No Kidding

Angie looked at all the gifts her father got for Father's Day and said, "When is it going to be Little Girl's Day, Mommy?"

"There isn't a Little Girl's Day, honey."

"But, Mommy, there has to be a day for boys and girls too."

Mommy probably thought, *Every day is kids' day!*

How Times Change

Five-year-old Caitrin and I went to a local park after I'd traveled a long distance to visit her and her family. We had such a good time together playing on the equipment that Caitrin asked, "Grammy, can we go to the park every time you visit?"

"Of course we can," I agreed, knowing that in a short time she'd outgrow the park. But I loved that she wanted to make this our special place.

This year she turned fourteen. We did not go to the park. We played at the mall instead.

Hey, Good Lookin'

"Grandpa," Richie said, "Mom says you and I look alike."

"Really? That's a compliment 'cause you're one good-lookin' boy."

Richie paused. "She was showing me a picture of you when you were little."

"Nice to hear," said Grandpa. "What else did your mom say?"

"Grandpa's changed a lot."

Worth a Thousand Words

My granddaughter Johannah and her family moved from Southern California to Ohio when she was about ten years old. A few days before they drove off with all their possessions, Johannah and I sat at the dining table in her house and did some art work. She turned out a beautifully colored drawing of herself, including her lovely blue eyes and long red hair. I nearly wept when I looked at it.

"Here, Grammy," she said, handing it to me to keep. "This is so you won't forget me."

As if I could!

A Note from the Editors

We hope you enjoy *Grandkids Say the Cutest Things* by Karen O'Connor, specially selected by the editors of the Books and Inspirational Media Division of Guideposts, a nonprofit organization that touches millions of lives every day through products and services that inspire, encourage, help you grow in your faith, and celebrate God's love in every aspect of your daily life.

Thank you for making a difference with your purchase of this book, which helps fund our many outreach programs to military personnel, prisons, hospitals, nursing homes, and educational institutions. To learn more, visit GuidepostsFoundation.org.

We also maintain many useful and uplifting online resources. Visit Guideposts.org to read true stories of hope and inspiration, access OurPrayer network, sign up for free newsletters, download free e-books, join our Facebook community, and follow our stimulating blogs.

To learn about other Guideposts publications, including the best-selling devotional *Daily Guideposts*, go to ShopGuideposts.org, call (800) 932-2145, or write to Guideposts, PO Box 5815, Harlan, Iowa 51593.